Excel 2019 Conditional Formatting

EASY EXCEL ESSENTIALS 2019 BOOK 3

M.L. HUMPHREY

SELECT TITLES BY M.L. HUMPHREY

EASY EXCEL ESSENTIALS 2019

Excel 2019 PivotTables

Excel 2019 Charts

Excel 2019 Conditional Formatting

Excel 2019 The IF Functions

EXCEL ESSENTIALS 2019

Excel 2019 Beginner

Excel 2019 Intermediate

Excel 2019 Formulas & Functions

ACCESS ESSENTIALS

Access for Beginners

Intermediate Access

CONTENTS

Introduction

The *Easy Excel Essentials 2019* series of titles are for intermediate-level users who want to focus on one specific topic such as PivotTables, Charts, Conditional Formatting, or the IF Functions.

The content of each title is extracted from either *Excel 2019 Intermediate* or *Excel 2019 Formulas & Functions* which cover intermediate-level Excel topics in more detail.

These books are written using Excel 2019 and assuming that a user is working in that program. If you are using an older version of Excel, the *Easy Excel Essentials* series may be a better choice since it was written using Excel 2013 and for a more general audience of Excel users.

With that introduction, let's dive in on how to use Conditional Formatting.

Conditional Formatting

What is conditional formatting and why would you want to use it?

At its most basic, conditional formatting is a set of rules you can apply to your data that help you see when certain criteria have been met.

I, for example, use it in my budget worksheet where I list my bank account values. I have minimum balance requirements on my checking and savings accounts, so both of the cells where I list those minimum required balances are set up with conditional formatting that will color those cells red if the balance in either account drops below the minimum requirement.

This helps remind me of those requirements, because I'm not always thinking about them when I move money around.

Another example of how to use conditional formatting would be if you track payments people owe you in Excel. You could either set up conditional formatting to flag when a payment is more than 30 days past its due date or when the date is outside of a specified range.

Conditional formatting is also useful when you have a set of data and want to easily flag certain results as good or bad. In my prior career I had to look for customer transactions where the customer paid a commission of over 5%. Sometimes there were thousands of lines of data, but I could have set up a conditional formatting rule that shaded any value over 5% red which would have made it very easy to scan my results and see the ones that were too high.

Even better, you can actually combine conditional formatting with filtering so that you first apply your conditional formatting (in this case turning all values over 5% red) and then your filter the data using Cell Color or Font Color so that you're only seeing the rows with data that was flagged.

The easiest way to see how conditional formatting works is to walk through an example. So let's do that.

Highlight Cells Rules

One of my favorite things to create in Excel is a two-variable analysis grid. This takes one item, say price, and puts it across the top of a table. And then takes another item, say units sold, and puts that down the side of the table. The center of the table is then a calculation of the result for all possible combinations of your two variables.

Here is one I already built that calculates the amount earned at various combinations of price and units sold.

		Price				
		$1	$2	$3	$4	$5
Units	10	$10	$20	$30	$40	$50
	25	$25	$50	$75	$100	$125
	100	$100	$200	$300	$400	$500
	500	$500	$1,000	$1,500	$2,000	$2,500

See the prices along the top and the units along the side and how at the intersection of each price and unit combination the value is the price multiplied times the number of units?

Now. Let's say that you need to earn at least $500 in order to make a profit on selling whatever this product is. There are a number of ways to do that. You could sell 500 units for $1. You could sell 100 units for $5.

It's possible to just look through the values and manually identify the ones that are over $500, but this is where conditional formatting can be incredibly helpful.

We're now going to apply shading to those calculated values so that we can quickly and easily see each value that is $500 or more.

First step, highlight the cells we want to apply our formatting to.

Next, we go the Styles section of the Home tab and click on the arrow under Conditional Formatting to see the dropdown menu.

We're going to choose the first option in that dropdown which is Highlight Cells Rules. If you hold your mouse over that text it will bring up a secondary dropdown menu with a large variety of choices.

Specifically, you can choose from Greater Than, Less Than, Between, Equal To, Text That Contains, A Date Occurring, and Duplicate Values. There's also a More Rules option at the bottom that will bring up the New Formatting Rule dialogue box. But for now we're going to choose Greater Than.

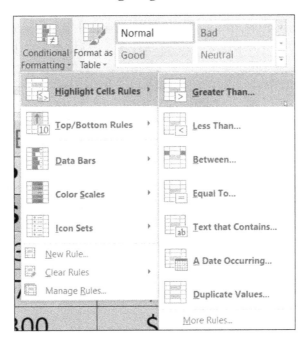

This brings up the Greater Than dialogue box which has two inputs. On the left-hand side you specify the value that you want to use for your greater than condition and on the right-hand side you choose the type of format you want to apply to your cells if that condition is met.

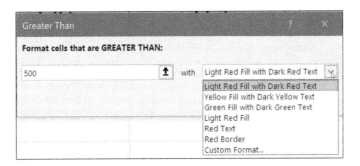

In the screenshot above I have actually made an error in what I chose. Because this is a GREATER THAN condition which means if I enter 500 then only values above 500 will be formatted the way I want. What I need to enter is 499.99 instead.

You can't see it here, but as you enter your values in the dialogue box and choose your formatting Excel will apply that formatting to the worksheet so you can see what the result is going to be before you give the final OK. In a scenario like this one where I want to flag the good results I usually use the Green Fill with Dark Green Text option because green = good, red = bad, at least in the U.S.

For a basic, simple analysis like this one the Light Red Fill with Dark Red Text and the Green Fill with Dark Green Text options usually do all you need. But there is a Custom Format option at the bottom of that dropdown that will let you apply pretty much any formatting you want via the Format Cells dialogue box.

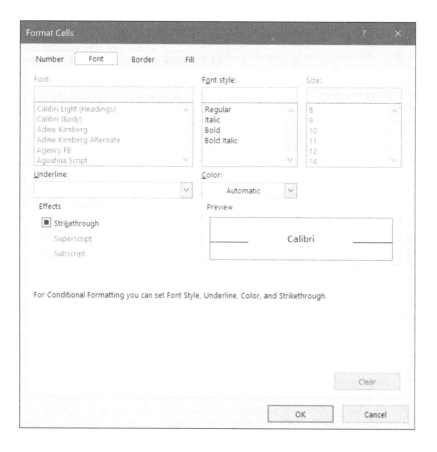

Font and Font Size are grayed out, but borders, fill color, font style, number format, etc. are all available.

I was just able to choose to format my text with a purple font and in italics. But let's just change that back to Green with Green and click OK.

Here we are:

		Price				
		$1	$2	$3	$4	$5
Units	**10**	$10	$20	$30	$40	$50
	25	$25	$50	$75	$100	$125
	100	$100	$200	$300	$400	$500
	500	$500	$1,000	$1,500	$2,000	$2,500

Compare this to our earlier version of the grid and you can see that there are now six cells that have shading on them. (And if this were in color you'd see that they are green with green text.)

All six of those cells meet our condition of being equal to or greater than $499.99. Now,with a simple glance we can see what combinations of price and units get us to our goal.

The other options in that Highlight Cells Rules dropdown work basically the exact same way. Each one you select will bring up a dialogue box where you input your parameter and select your formatting. The only real difference is what type of analysis it's doing. (Greater Than, Less Than, etc.)

The duplicate values option is a little weird because it doesn't discriminate between different values. In our sample data table we have two cells with a value of $50, two cells with a value of $100, and two cells with a value of $500. If I select the cells in my data table and tell Excel to highlight duplicate values, this is what I get:

		Price				
		$1	$2	$3	$4	$5
Units	**10**	$10	$20	$30	$40	$50
	25	$25	$50	$75	$100	$125
	100	$100	$200	$300	$400	$500
	500	$500	$1,000	$1,500	$2,000	$2,500

Even though there are three separate values that are duplicated, all six cells with duplicate values are formatted the exact same way.

I personally don't find that tremendously useful because I then still have to distinguish between the $50, $100, and $500 values. Most times when I'm looking for duplicates it is so I can eliminate one (or more) entry with the same value.

The date option is a bit odd as well because you can't specify a date or date range to use. It only lets you flag a date occurring yesterday, today, tomorrow, in the last seven days, last week, this week, next week, last month, this month, or next month.

Depending on what you want to use it for, those options could be very useful or very limited.

Top/Bottom Rules

The next set of conditional formatting rules you can use are called Top/Bottom Rules.

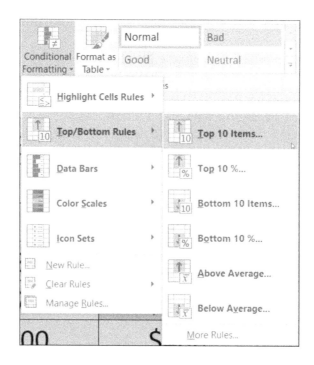

With the Top/Bottom Rules, you can format values that fall in the top X of your range (like top 10), the bottom X of your range, the top X% of your range, the bottom X% of your range, above the average for the range, or below the average for the range.

(While the options are labeled Top 10 Items, Top 10%, etc. when you click on them you'll see that you can adjust the number to whatever you want to use.)

For example, here is the Top 10 items dialogue box.

In the screenshot above you can see that I've changed the value so that it will format the top 16 values instead of the top 10. You can use the arrows there next to the number or click into the box and type in the number you want.

As with the Highlight Cells Rules you have the same set of preset dropdown format options or can choose Custom Format at the bottom of the list.

Data Bars

Data bars are where things start to get interesting. Up until now you could have technically gone through and manually formatted your data to get the same effect as the highlight cells rules or the top/bottom rules.

(It would be a bad idea, because conditional formatting adjusts with your data whereas manually doing that exact same formatting to flag values only works if your data never changes again. But technically they'd *look* the same in that moment in time.)

Data bars, however, place a bar in each cell where the length of the bar is determined by how big the value in that cell is compared to all other values in the selected range.

Your options in the secondary dropdown menu are mostly just formatting-related options. You can choose different default colors, namely blue, green, red, orange, light blue, and purple. And you can choose between a solid bar and a gradient bar.

The easiest way to see the difference between the solid and the gradient option is to look at it. So let's do that. In the screenshot below the gradient option is on the left-hand side and the solid option is on the right-hand side. Both of these were done in the "light blue" color.

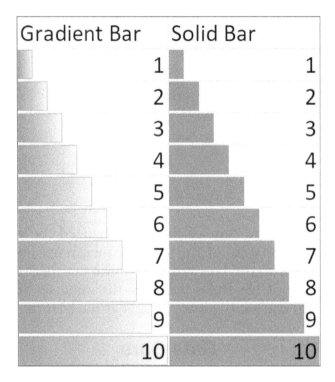

With data bars you can change the settings so that only the bar shows and the number is hidden, but we'll talk about that in a moment after we talk about Color Scales and Icon Sets.

Color Scales

Color Scales is one I actually use quite often. I have an Excel spreadsheet that shows the amount of revenue I've earned each month as well as the amount I've spent on ads each month and for each of those columns I have color scales applied that quickly show me the months where I either earned the most or spent the most.

So what do color scales do? They color a cell a shade of color along a spectrum based upon the relative value in that cell compared to the rest of the range.

Just like with data bars, the secondary dropdown menu on this one is basically preset color choices. You have red/yellow/green, red/white/green, red/white/blue, shades of red, shades of green, and green/yellow and you can choose those to go in either direction.

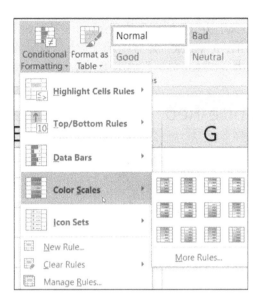

What I mean by that is that you can, for example with the red/yellow/green option shade the smallest values red and the largest values green or you can shade the smallest values green and the largest values red. It all depends on what is "good" or "bad" in your particular scenario.

I will add a comment here to be careful about color-coding when your color choices are arbitrary. For example, that red/white/blue option is meaningless to me. Red and green are commonly used together to represent "bad" and "good" results but when you replace green with blue my mind does not automatically assume that blue is bad so then I'm left looking at shaded cells and wondering what to make of it.

In another scenario I saw recently someone had used shading that was applied to values ranging from -100 to 100. Zero was neutral, -100 was good, 100 was bad. But they had used just one color so it was all shades of red which made the zero results, which were neutral, look like they were bad results. In that example, the green/yellow/red scale or something like it would've been a better choice.

We'll get into customization in a moment, but this is one where I like to choose a custom color to use for my scales just because I find the default choices of red and green boring.

Another thing to keep in mind with this one is that you may have to change your font color for the larger values because black text does not always show well with the darker cell shading.

Real quick, here is an example of the difference between the white-red color scale option and the red-white color scale option. As you can see, the white-red option made the cell with a value of 10 in it the white cell and the red-white option made the cell with a value of 1 in it the white cell.

White-Red	Red-White
1	1
2	2
3	3
4	4
5	5
6	6
7	7
8	8
9	9
10	10

Icon Sets

Your last option is Icon Sets which are an interesting one because they insert a symbol into each cell based on its relative value within the range. You can see your icon choices in the secondary menu after you select Icon Sets.

There are a number of icon sets to choose from that will group your data into three-part, four-part, or five-part categories and will use various shapes such as arrows, circles, etc. to do so.

In the following screenshot I've used four of the options to show you how they differ based upon shape and number of levels. I've labeled each column according to the description that Excel uses. (You can see the name Excel has assigned to each icon set by holding your mouse over it in the secondary dropdown menu.)

Five Quarters		4 Ratings		3 Triangles		3 Symbols Circled	
○	1	⊿	1	▼	1	⊗	1
○	2	⊿	2	▼	2	⊗	2
◔	3	⊿	3	▼	3	⊗	3
◔	4	⊿	4	▬	4	◑	4
◐	5	⊿	5	▬	5	◑	5
◐	6	⊿	6	▬	6	◑	6
◕	7	⊿	7	▬	7	◑	7
◕	8	⊿	8	▲	8	✓	8
●	9	⊿	9	▲	9	✓	9
●	10	⊿	10	▲	10	✓	10

So a wide variety of choices.

In Excel 2019 if you use icon sets on your data you can then filter your data by each icon. It's under the Filter By Color option. Pull up the secondary menu there and you'll see your icons listed as filter choices under the heading Filter by Cell Icon.

Customization

What we just walked through are the defaults. But you can customize your data ranges and your formats much more than that.

If you want to use Data Bars, Color Scales, or Icon Sets but you want to set absolute limits for when a format is applied (as opposed to letting Excel look at the data and divide it evenly), you can do so by applying default rules and then choosing Manage Rules from the Conditional Formatting dropdown in the Styles section of the Home tab. This will bring up the Conditional Formatting Rules Manager.

The dialogue box will default to Current Selection and only show you the rules that exist for that cell or range of cells, but you can change the dropdown to This Worksheet to see all of the rules that exist in your worksheet.

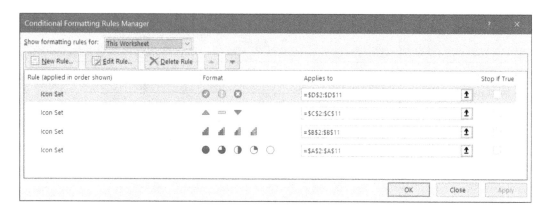

In the screenshot above I have four sets of conditional formatting rules in this worksheet, each applied to a different range of cells.

Note that you can apply more than one conditional formatting rule to a specific cell. When you do that, you can tell Excel by checking the checkboxes on the right-hand side to stop if one of the rules is true and then not apply the rest of the rules.

You can also change the order of your rules using those arrows in the section directly above the rule listing. Just click on the rule you want to move first.

In the past I've had conditional formatting rules where I wanted different formatting on different value ranges and so I had a rule that was >100, say, and then a rule that was >50, etc. Because of how they were written, with that > operator and the overlap in potential results where a value of 150 would be both >100 and >50, the order of the rules mattered.

In this scenario that we're looking at here, it doesn't. There's no overlap across the cell ranges.

So back to customization.

Choose the rule you want to customize, click on its row, and then choose Edit Rule. That will bring up the Edit Formatting Rule dialogue box which will already be completed with the defaults that Excel chose for you when your initially created the rule.

Let's look at an example.

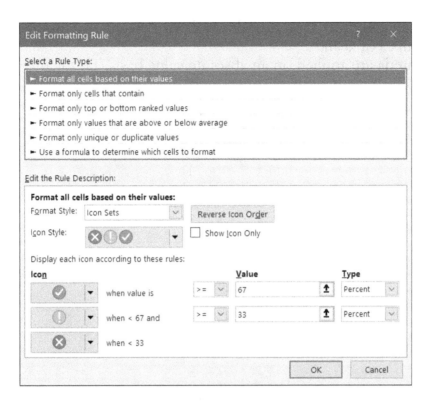

So you can see here that I've chosen an icon set rule that has three categories, the X, the exclamation mark, and the checkmark. Because of that Excel has divided my results on a percent basis where the bottom third of the values are the X, the next third are the exclamation mark, and the final third are the checkmark.

I can change this. So let's say that I want absolute values. Anything 6 and above gets a checkmark, anything under 2 gets an X, and anything in between gets the exclamation mark.

I do that by changing the Type dropdown from Percent to Number and then entering my values of 6 and 2.

Now the criteria are applied on an absolute value basis. This is the result:

3 Symbols Circled
✖ 1
◯ 2
◯ 3
◯ 4
◯ 5
✔ 6
✔ 7
✔ 8
✔ 9
✔ 10

See the difference? There's now only one X in the whole table because there's only one value below 2 and the 6 and 7 values now have a check next to them instead of an exclamation mark.

Be careful of your edge cases. In this scenario the 6 and the 2.

Because I used >= as my rule for both, that meant that the 2 value was not given an X. If I'd wanted values of 2 or less to be an X, then I would've needed to change that option to > only. (That's the only other choice you have.)

I usually forget to pay attention to that and have to go back and fix it later. If you're like me, be sure to always test those values in your data when you set up your conditional formatting.

In the Edit Formatting Rule dialogue box you can also change the icon set you're using or, actually, change anything about your conditional formatting.

Here's the top portion of that dialogue box:

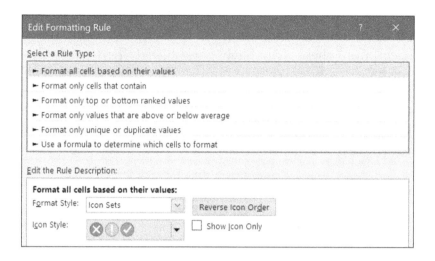

First, see at the bottom where it says Icon Style and there's a dropdown? You can click there and select any of the other icon set options.

To the right of that is a checkbox where you can click to Show Icon Only. This will keep the shapes or the bars or whatever, but it will hide the actual value.

Above that you can reverse the icon order so that the value that was "bad" before is now "good."

And then above that if you read those options in Select Rule Type you'll see that you can change this conditional formatting rule to any of the other options. For example, the third option there, format only top and bottom ranked values is the Top/Bottom Rules.

The dropdowns we walked through before were the shortcuts that Excel has put in place to make it easy to do the most common formatting. But here you have almost complete control.

Remove Conditional Formatting

What do you do if you've added conditional formatting and you want to remove it? You can go back to the Conditional Formatting dropdown and choose Clear Rules from the bottom section. This will show you a secondary dropdown that says Clear Rules from Selected Cells or Clear Rules from Entire Sheet. (There are two other options there about clearing rules from tables or PivotTables that will only be available if that applies in your situation.)

If you've selected the cells with the formatting that you want to remove, just choose Clear Rules from Selected Cells.

If you're not sure where you have conditional formatting and want it all removed from the worksheet you can choose Clear Rules from Entire Sheet.

The other option is to select Manage Rules. This brings up the Conditional Formatting Rule Manager and you can then see all rules that exist for that selection or any worksheet in the entire file. To remove one of those rules, click on the rule to select it and then click Delete Rule from the section above the rules.

Extend a Covered Range of Cells

There are probably other ways to do this, but when I have a range of cells that have conditional formatting on them and I add to the values but my new values are not included in the formatting range, I go to the Manage Rules option to fix this.

It's tempting to think that you can use the Format Painter to do this—just click on one of the cells with your conditional formatting and then click on the new cell range. But the problem with doing so is that Excel treats those new cells as a new range. So the formatting transfers, but the range you had before and the new range are evaluated separately.

For an absolute value scenario like the one we created above, that's not a problem. For a relative value scenario, it is. See here:

	5	5
▲	6	6
▲	7	7
▼	8	8
	9	9
▲	10	10

What I did for both of these columns is remove the conditional formatting from the cells for 8, 9, and 10 and then reapplied it using Format Painter.

The example on the left is one where the conditional formatting rule is relative. The bottom 1/3 of values get a down arrow, the middle 1/3 get a bar, and the top 1/3 get an up arrow.

You can see here that 8, 9, and 10 were treated as their own group for purposes of assigning an icon which is why the 8 has a down arrow and the 9 has a bar even though they are in a column of numbers ranging from 1 through 10.

The column on the right is the one we edited earlier where we had absolute values in our criteria. Any value 6 or above got a checkmark. Using Format Painter in this scenario worked because the criteria are absolute.

Rather than go through that mental gymnastics, I just always use the Manage Rules option to extend my cell range. Although that can have its issues as well.

To do this, go to the Conditional Formatting dropdown in the Styles section of the Home tab and choose Manage Rules. This will let you see each rule and the cell range it applies to. (In the Applies To column.)

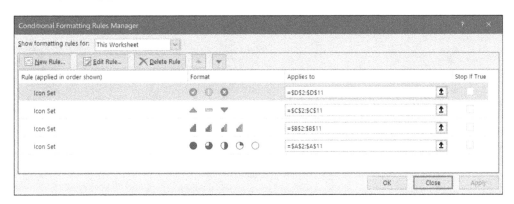

If you're just extending a range, click into that box, backspace to delete the current last row value and type in the new row value and then hit enter. If you want to put a second, non-continuous cell range, you can do so by using a comma and typing in the new range.

This approach works well as long as you don't try using the arrow keys. Click into that box and use the arrow key and Excel tries to be helpful and gives you the next cell in your worksheet from the one you had selected when you opened the dialogue box. It basically erases what was already in there and replaces it with a cell selection you don't want.

(Ctrl + Z , undo, is your friend when things like that happen.)

There is also an arrow with a bar under it at the end of the listed cell range. You can click on that and it will show you in the worksheet which cells the formatting currently applies to. You can then click into your worksheet and highlight the cells you want it to apply to and you'll see a small dialogue box that updates with the new range. Hit enter when you're done with your selection and it will update.

Conclusion

Alright. That was conditional formatting. If you want to learn more niche topics, check out the rest of the series which covers PivotTables, Charts, and the IF Functions. Or if you want to now explore a broader range of topics you can choose *Excel 2019 Intermediate* or *Excel 2019 Formulas & Functions* which cover those topics and more.

Appendix A: Basic Terminology

Most of the terminology I use is pretty standard but I think I do have a few quirks in how I refer to things, so be sure to do a quick skim of this section just to make sure we're on the same page. This is meant to be a refresher only. These terms were initially taught in *Excel 2019 Beginner*.

Column

Excel uses columns and rows to display information. Columns run across the top of the worksheet and, unless you've done something funky with your settings, are identified using letters of the alphabet.

Row

Rows run down the side of the worksheet and are numbered starting at 1 and up to a very high number. In Excel 2019 that number is 1048576.

Cell

A cell is a combination of a column and row that is identified by the letter of the column it's in and the number of the row it's in. For example, Cell A1 is the cell in the first column and first row of a worksheet.

Click

If I tell you to click on something, that means to use your mouse (or trackpad) to move the cursor on the screen over to a specific location and left-click or right-click on the option. (See the next definition for the difference between left-click and right-click).

If you left-click, this generally selects the item. If you right-click, this generally creates a dropdown list of options to choose from. If I don't tell you which to do, left- or right-click, then left-click.

Left-click/Right-click

If you look at your mouse or your trackpad, you generally have two flat buttons to press. One is on the left side, one is on the right. If I say left-click that means to press down on the button on the left. If I say right-click that means press down on the button on the right. (If you're used to using Word or Excel you may already do this without even thinking about it. If that's the case then think of left-click as what you usually use to select text and right-click as what you use to see a menu of choices.)

Spreadsheet

I'll try to avoid using this term, but if I do use it, I'll mean your entire Excel file. It's a little confusing because it can sometimes also be used to mean a specific worksheet, which is why I'll try to avoid it as much as possible.

Worksheet

This is the term I'll use as much as possible. A worksheet is a combination of rows and columns that you can enter data in. When you open an Excel file, it opens to Sheet1.

Workbook

I don't use this term often, but it may come up. A workbook is an Excel file and can contain multiple worksheets. The default file type for an Excel 2019 workbook is a .xlsx file type.

Formula Bar

This is the long white bar at the top of the screen with the $f\chi$ symbol next to it.

Tab

I refer to the menu choices at the top of the screen (File, Home, Insert, Page Layout, Formulas, Data, Review, View, and Help) as tabs. Note how they look like folder tabs from an old-time filing system when selected? That's why.

Data

I use data and information interchangeably. Whatever information you put into a worksheet is your data or data set.

Select

If I tell you to "select" cells, that means to highlight them. Same with text.

Arrow

If I say that you can "arrow" to something that just means to use the arrow keys to navigate from one cell to another.

Cell Notation

We may end up talking about cell ranges in this book. Excel uses a very specific type of cell notation. We already mentioned that a cell is referenced based upon the letter of its column and the number of its row. So A1 is the cell in Column A and Row 1. (When used as cell notation you don't need to include Cell before the A1.)

To reference a range of cells Excel uses the colon (:) and the comma (,). A colon between cells means "through". So A1:B25 means all of the cells between Cell A1 and Cell B25 which is all of the cells in Columns A and B and Rows 1 through 25. A comma means and. So A1,B25 would be Cells A1 and B25 only.

When in doubt, go into Excel, type = and the cell range, hit enter, and then double-click back into that cell. Excel will highlight all of the cells in the range you entered.

Dialogue Box

I will sometimes refer to dialogue boxes. These are the boxes that occasionally pop up with additional options for you to choose from for a particular task.

Paste Special – Values

Paste Special - Values is a special type of pasting option which I often use to remove formulas from my data or to remove a pivot table but keep the table it created. If I tell you to Paste Special - Values that means use the Values paste option which is the one with a 123 on the clipboard.

Dropdown

I will occasionally refer to a dropdown or dropdown menu. This is generally a list of potential choices that you can select from if you right-click on your worksheet or on one of the arrows next to an option in the tabs at the top. For example, if you go to the Home tab and click on the arrow under Paste, you will see additional options listed in a paste dropdown menu.

Task Pane

I am going to call the separate standalone pane that appears on the right-hand side of the screen on occasion a task pane. These appear for PivotTables, charts, and the Help function.

About the Author

M.L. Humphrey is a former stockbroker with a degree in Economics from Stanford and an MBA from Wharton who has spent close to twenty years as a regulator and consultant in the financial services industry.

You can reach M.L. Humphrey at:

mlhumphreywriter@gmail.com

or at

www.mlhumphrey.com

www.ingramcontent.com/pod-product-compliance
Lightning Source LLC
Chambersburg PA
CBHW060513060326
40689CB00020B/4732